FROM THE CREATORS OF THE INTERNATIONAL BEST-SELLER WHY CATS PAINT

# DANCING WITH CATS

Burton Silver & Heather Busch

WEIDENFELD
& NICOLSON

London

First published in the United States in 1999 by
Chronicle Books.

First published in Great Britain in 1999
by Weidenfeld & Nicolson

A CIP catalogue record for this book is available
from the British Library

ISBN 0 297 82530 5

Editorial: Melissa da Souza
Layout design: Heather Busch

Neither the publisher, author nor photographer
accept any responsibility for any adverse reactions
which may result from the use of material in this
book. No cats were harmed during the creation of
this book.

*Dancing with Cats* is a registered international
experiment in inter-species morphic resonance and
is designed to test the hypothesis of formative causa-
tion. I.E.# 99-306810-7.

Printed in Hong Kong

Weidenfeld & Nicolson
The Orion Publishing Group Ltd
Orion House
5 Upper Saint Martin's Lane
London WC2H 9EA

Cover Illustration: Wiky and Arijá harmonize during a witty *diver-
tissement* entitled *Zen Zoom*. Illustration page 2: Selena's "fairy chant"
creates the perfect ambience for Zoot's *glissades*. Illustration this
page: *pas de deux, pas de chat.*

# CONTENTS

# FOREWORD

FOR some years now, a new consciousness has been entering our world, a new understanding of the energy fields that tie us and all living things together. More particularly, there is a growing awareness that the animals we share our lives with are a dynamic part of these fields of energy and that they can influence how we humans feel and act.

Fresh insights into these transcendent fields have focused on the mysterious psychic abilities displayed by domestic cats. For centuries, these have been explained away as mere coincidences, and therefore of no significance—or have been put down as the work of evil forces. But when we consider how the psychic energy of the cat has been able to affect so many lives in positive ways, we begin to understand that cats possess special gifts, a spiritual dimension that cannot be lightly dismissed. Why, for example, do those who have a close relationship with their cats recover more quickly from serious illnesses? How is it that some cats know the precise moment their owner leaves to come home; and why does your cat sometimes come running to you just seconds after you've thought about him or her? We cannot examine these facts without beginning to see direct evidence of some kind of mysterious force at work—a dynamic energy flowing between ourselves and our cats.

By tuning in to this feline power, more and more people are experiencing a kind of spiritual partnership with their cats, an interaction on a deeper, more vibrant plane. In my experience, one of the best methods of achieving this is by dancing with cats. Magnifying bio-energy vibrations through deep communication and synchronicity of movement, this most exciting of activities produces intense feelings of empowerment and validation.

It only remains for us to open our minds and allow the personal testimonies and inspirational photographs that follow to guide us toward a new spiritual unfolding.

Swami Shakya Bahrain,
Spiritual Healer

Opposite:
One of the world's most accomplished cat dancers, Arijá Davies dances with Petipa. Arijá's high levels of etheric energy enable her to dance with a wide variety of cats.

# PREFACE

THIS book almost didn't happen. Frustrated after months of attempting to photograph people dancing with their cats, we were ready to give up after yet another photo shoot was stymied by the refusal of the cat to perform in front of a camera. Although we had been treated to several tantalizing displays of interspecies dance, any attempts to capture them on film were met by feline disdain. We decided that cat dancing was a private affair which could not withstand the intrusion of spectators or cameras. Thankfully, just at that point, we met up with Arijá Davies.

Just seventeen years old, Arijá (pronounced "aria") was already an accomplished cat dancer, not only with her cat but with others' cats as well. She was happy to dance for us, and her lovely ginger tom, Nijinskat, was remarkably relaxed about our presence. Better still, Arijá was one of a group of women who met at each other's houses to dance with their cats and swap ideas. As a result, their cats were less sensitive to an audience. They not only continued their dancing, but also remained unperturbed as we moved into their homes with the backdrops and lighting required to capture the images that would do justice to this remarkable activity. Arijá and her friends are part of a revival in cat dancing which seems to have spread from New Zealand and the US in the late eighties to Europe and other parts of the world in the early nineties. What actually stimulated this revival is not known, but it is clearly part of a general trend away from materialism toward a more spiritual appreciation of our hidden instincts and powers. We met some people who began cat dancing spontaneously and genuinely believed they had invented it. But dancing with cats is not a new phenomenon.

The earliest written record of a cat dancing with a person dates from 1692 and evidence of the practice is alluded to in the nursery rhyme *Hey diddle diddle.* "The cat and the fiddle" is clearly a reference to the cat's supposed ability to somehow get us up and dancing, even causing "the dish" (the maid) to run away with the "spoon" (a crazy person). References like this from the Middle Ages are almost always derogatory, as the church encouraged the belief that "those who durst jig by the cat do cavort with the devil hemself." Indeed, there is little doubt that it was women swishing their brooms in front of cats in order to excite them to dance, so they could join them and attain "higher states and magic cures," that led to the absurd notion of witches riding aloft on broomsticks with their cats.

In this enlightened age, dancing with cats no longer attracts anti-pagan scrutiny, but there still remains a good deal of controversy surrounding the reasons why cats dance with us. Biologist Desmond Morris, in his book

*Catlore*, explains the "mad dashes" that cats make as "overflow or vacuum activities" that enable the cat, especially if it is kept indoors, "to release some of its hunting or fleeing energy and feel more relaxed again." But cat dancers say many dancing cats aren't kept indoors and the explanation doesn't account for the fact that it is sometimes the cat, rather than its human partner, that actively initiates the dance. Indeed, Desmond Morris notes "a cat may approach its human owner and purposely make a nuisance of itself in a way it has learned will cause anger. When the owner shouts at the cat, instead of simply stopping as it usually does, the cat will massively overreact with one of its mad-panic rushes." Whether this is an attempt by the cat to provoke us into dancing rather than, as biologists maintain, a simple release of energy is unclear. What is clear is that those who accept the invitation and become willing partners in the dance are profoundly affected, physically and emotionally.

It is our hope that this book will encourage others to experience that uplifting energy by dancing with their cats and, in so doing, help facilitate a greater understanding between us humans and our feline companions.

Burton Silver & Heather Busch, 1999

Cats perform integrated whiplash leaps during a *pas de trois*.

9

# INTRODUCTION

E will probably never know for sure why cats dance with us. We do know that some kind of energy is released in the process that can have a profound effect on human beings and probably on cats as well. It seems that by synchronizing our movements, no matter how briefly, with those of the cat, we momentarily bring our energy fields together, creating a whole new vitality which feeds back into and invigorates the two original fields. The greater the unity of movement, the more intense the dynamic. Of course, we don't know what cats ultimately gain from the experience, but the human gain is well documented.

First there are the physiological effects. Cat dancers report a variety of physical sensations that range from "pleasant tingling and lightheadedness" to "whole body spasm and uncontrolled muscle quiver." Such effects make it seem likely that the feline energy system is influencing the human system on a neuro-muscular level.

The psychological effects are, however, more difficult to explain. Dancers universally claim strong positive emotions are triggered by synchronized interaction with their cats. Whenever we do anything in unison with others it usually engenders some feelings of unity and togetherness which result in heightened perceptions of personal worth. But there is something more powerful occurring here.

Not only do dancers talk of "feeling alive for the first time," but they also say the feeling lasts for days. Some even claim major personality shifts, stating that they no longer suffer from depression and have become more outgoing, assertive, and generous.

Few people are blessed with the innate ability to communicate quickly on a deep level with a wide variety of cats—people such as Arijá Davies, for instance, who is featured throughout this book and is able to dance with a cat she has never met before after only a brief acquaintance. Most of us must be prepared to put in several hours of pre-dance work with our cats. This may include noncontact stroking, mutual nuzzling and rubbing, prone mirroring, and occasional washing imitations before we get any results at all. Unless, of course, we are lucky enough to own a cat who initiates the dance itself by rushing about in order to provoke us into joining it in an energy building experience. The sad thing is that most people do not recognize this display for the invitation it is. Instead of gladly taking the opportunity to dance with their cat, they dismiss it as some kind of dysfunctional feline behavior.

Building a successful relationship with your cat which will result in fruitful dance experiences is largely dependent on your own mental and spiritual preparation. You need to be free of skepticism and totally committed to the interaction. Cats are able to detect any ambivalence on your part and will refrain from dancing with you until you have liberated yourself from the negativity of self-conscious doubt. It is precisely because of their lack of self-consciousness that children are able to form dance relationships with cats more quickly.

The fact that cats dance more easily with us when there is musical accompaniment may have more to do with the way music releases us into the dance than the cats' actual enjoyment of it. However, some cats do seem to prefer certain kinds of music and it is worth experimenting to find out what music your cat likes best. You can do this by noticing whether it nods its head or swishes its tail in time to the music. Moreover, if you have no objection to your cat taking performance-enhancing drugs, you might like to try making catnip or valerian available before a dance session.

There are two main methods people use to initiate a dance rapport with their cats. Some begin by holding their cat in their arms while gently moving to their favorite music. Once your cat starts to purr, which is its way of modulating energy, you know that its vibratory levels are being raised in readiness for alignment with yours. At this point you can place it on the ground and begin to sway and move around it in time to the music. Others, using a technique called mirroring, mimic their cat's every move as a means of bringing their energy levels into sympathetic contact. With both these methods, there comes a point

where the cat reciprocates and synchronizes its movement with yours in a joyous explosion of energy release.

Our worldview has changed radically in the last fifty years. Relativity and quantum theory have enabled us to see all animals and plants not as complex machines, but rather as intricate networks of energy fields which coexist in some kind of dynamic interplay with our cellular systems. Dancing with cats clearly demonstrates that these energies are able to link up and provide not only a new vitality, but also, on a deeper level, a way of exploring new spiritual insights that will guide us in the third millennium.

OR Ralph, the actual dance itself always begins with The Invitation. "I come right down to the cat's level and begin purring really loudly. Then I push one foot out behind like a tail and flick it from side to side in the feline 'let's go' signal. At the same time, I reach out for Petipa's paw, stop purring, and begin to hum something that seems just right for the moment. It could be one of Handel's oratorios or a sprightly chakra cha cha. The faster it is, the higher Petipa leaps."

*"Don't ask if your cat will dance with you—will you dance with your cat?"*

13

$\mathcal{P}$ETIPA responds with vigor equal to Ralph's robust song and flamboyant gestures. Once the energy level is raised, Ralph feels that his postures become imbued with an unconscious spiritual significance which Petipa affirms by countering with her own complementary moves. A hopping arabesque from Ralph may provoke a series of elegant stalking leaps from Petipa, while a fluttering of fingers may be countered with tiny aerial flurries. Poignant moments of unconcerned fur licking puntuate the patterns of the dance.

15

*W*HEN Ralph dances with two cats, the energy fields can become confused. Instead of power being released through well-controlled movements, one cat tends to make sudden mad dashes and leaps. Cats who do this on their own are often good dancers.

A MOMENT of real empathy: Arijá sweeps low, sleek, and catlike, while Ginger mimics an upright two-legged human strut. "There are times during our dances when we become each other—when we're transformed. To dance with your cat you must be prepared for transformation. Only that inner willingness can bring the dance alive and give it real power," Arijá says.

"During our dances...we become each other."

*N*IJINSKAT follows his tail in a series of tight elevated turns and surging *sissonnes*. Cats respond well to visual images, and Arijá uses thought pictures to help coordinate the dance. "While I'm dancing, I picture Nijinskat in a certain position, and then imagine that image floating into his head like a bubble. For some reason he responds best when I color the whole image blue."

RIJÁ finds that interpreting a piece of classical ballet with her cat has emotional resonance. Her favorite is *Giselle*. "I'm always falling for men who aren't what they claim to be, so I identify strongly with Giselle. I start by lying on the floor and moaning softly. That's the sign for Nijinskat, who plays Albrecht, to leap over (*grand jeté*) and jump (*soubresant*) onto my back and begin purring and kneading all round my neck, as if he's urging me to turn my head and offer my lips. Ultimately, he fails; and I rise up like Giselle's ghost in act II and begin to spin around, symbolically unraveling the layers of my protective ego until I am revealed as pure spirit. Albrecht tries to connect with me by leaping up and waving desperately, but that me is not there anymore. I am disembodied, and he finishes by lying with his paw outstretched in a final rapacious entreaty. I bow low and *bourée* on out." Even though the whole *pas*

*de deux* lasts only a few minutes, Arijá claims that the *chi* levels are so intense she feels cleansed and re-created for days afterward. Nijinskat can hold chi energy by curling up and releasing it slowly through purring.

Following page: Nijinskat, the epitome of the *danseur noble*, shows off his spectacular technique in a free-ranging piece of contact improvisation with Arijá. Much of Nijinskat's eloquence is provided by the pure form of feline movement which, when unsullied by narrative interpretation, has the power to inspire the mind.

DAPHNE'S cat has displayed the ability to respond to her emotional states. "When things are bad I often console myself by singing and dancing nursery rhymes like we used to at school. Minstral has always been particularly attentive when I'm down, so I guess it was inevitable that one day he would join in. Now we dance Humpty Dumpty and Ding Dong Bell no matter what my mood. Minstral does a wonderful wobbly egg and is brilliant down the well." Through the joy of cat dancing, Daphne has become aware of our spiritual connection with animals and no longer eats meat. "You can't commune with animals and eat them, too," she says.

*"I dance out of my life for a few moments and come back inspired."*

*D*ANCING with a tail of his own attached, Fred becomes a psychic extension of the cat. "I share its grace, power, and oneness with the universe. I relate to Fluff and the whole spectrum of feline physicality on a profound level—I even regard birds differently."

*"The tail balances the body and restores psychic equilibrium."*     **29**

ELEN believes that Boots, her four-year-old Persian, dances so well with her because they share a lot in common. "He's a Scorpio and I have the sun in Pisces, so there's a good deal of karmic support. Also our auras usually match, and numerologically we're both Eights, which makes for a strong psychic bond." However, to ensure the correct energy balances, Helen finds that adjustments to the physical environment may be necessary. "I had the Feng-Shui cat-man in last year, and he had me place the cat-door in the living-room wall instead of the back door. That realignment really got Boots bunny hopping and stomping properly again."

*"When you dance with your cat you share in the gift of feline grace."*

BEFORE dancing, Helen and Boots do a series of mirroring exercises to specially developed feline soundscapes. They also spend time in noncontact stroking and mutual rubbing. "He rubs up against me and I rub up against him, and I feel fantastic! Don't let anybody tell you that cats rub up against you just to leave their scent on you. They do it because it builds up energy and makes them feel great and want to dance. My partner and I now regularly rub up against one another to reenergize and it's made a big difference to our relationship."

CAT dancing is likely a complex vocabulary of gestures that we have yet to recognize and fully understand. Helen, along with others who share her covenant, has come to feel that Boots's studied poses communicate his inner thoughts and embody his soul's unexpressed desires.

SOOTY twirls dervishly beneath Jane's swirling veil, responding with a series of graceful hip gyrations of her own. Jane's husband used to maintain that Sooty's jumping about was simply her excitement at the veil fluttering like a bird. But, Jane says, "When he saw her waggling her hips to the music, he had to admit pussy was really dancing." Jane thinks Sooty might be a reincarnated harem princess, or "maybe she somehow absorbed the moves from always sleeping on the pile of *Seventh Veil* magazines in the living room."

*Both veil and tail give balance, grace, and a spiritual sense of scale.*     **37**

TWO little newborn cardigans Joy found in the attic turned out to be irresistible to Pinkle (far left) and Tonk. The pink and blue jackets quickly became their favorite playthings and one day, when Joy dressed them up in them, the cats reacted in a most uncharacteristic way. "Tonk doesn't usually play with Pinkle, or vice versa," says Joy. "But with the cardigans on, they leapt all over each other like they were just thrilled to be together. Usually cats hate things on them, but Tonk especially is happy to wear hers all day." It was only recently that Joy learned that the jackets had been knitted for her great aunt and uncle who had lived in the Australian outback. They were extraordinarily close, never married, and spent all their lives together.

*"Cats can tell all about us by lying on our clothes."*

WHILE Pinkle and Tonk were happy to dance with each other, Pinkle always became more reserved when Joy attempted to join in. To overcome this, Joy tried dancing to a slow waltz while holding Pinkle in her arms. She discovered that by also gently stroking him in time to the music he would eventually respond by waving his front foot rhythmically. Joy could then put him down on the floor and he'd reenter the dance with his normal degree of exuberance.

INKLE and Tonk's dances often comprise a sequence of quite distinctive kangaroo leaps. All the power passes through the back legs while their front legs are held limply in front and hardly come in contact with the ground at all. Just what makes them suddenly begin this unusual bounding motion is not known.

WHEN Tonk dances with Joy's little sister, Jill, their movements are often remarkably synchronized. The girls' father believes that the younger the child, the quicker the bond, because cat and child share qualities of innocence and spontaneity, exuberance and unconditional love—qualities that are reflected in their dances together.

*S*UE, who actually teaches cat dancing, encourages her pupils to use their cat's greeting hop as an entrée to the dance. When their owners arrive home, many cats briefly rise up off their front legs and turn their heads to the side, aligning their energy patterns in a gesture of welcome. Gently guiding the cat's head around with your hand when it reaches the top of this greeting hop enables it to complete a full mid-air turn, *tour en l'air.* Once this is associated with music, most cats happily repeat the performance, especially when their owners also hop along with them.

B Y adopting the cat's very restful paw-droop pose, and bounding lightly up and down, Sue is able to tap into the profound energy of feline peace. For several magical moments, Tommy harmonizes his movements with hers to magnify their reciprocal energy. When a dance becomes perfectly synchronized it can produce a prolonged state of tranquillity in both feline and human, with interesting cognitive crossover effects.

"After a dance like that," says Sue, "I sleep for hours and dream of happy cat things, like scurrying mice and sweet, tasty little birds fluttering in the sun."

*"We dance with and in and through the power of the feline spirit."* **51**

SIMPLE way of improving the intuitive communication between you and your cat is to practice mirroring. First put on your cat's favorite music, and then adopt exactly the same position as the cat, but behind it so it can't see you. While breathing in time with your cat, begin to tap out the rhythm of the music with a finger. When you see the cat's tail or head also moving in time with the music, slowly raise a limb. If your cat mirrors your action, even only slightly, you know you've made vibrational contact. Zoot is particularly intuitive with very open energy channels. This makes him easy to "contact" in the dance and an excellent partner, who is sensitive to the give and take of collaborative artistic expression.

$S$UE puts on a bird costume in order to dance out some of her past traumas. "I adopt the form of the bird," she says, "because I want to feel vulnerable, like the naive little creature I once was—one who was preyed upon and abandoned by a charming but ultimately selfish male. Zoot treats me like he would a bird. He leaps about and showers me with attention, when in reality he only wants one thing—to dominate, consume, and move on." Dancing with Zoot helps Sue reenact and come to terms with the joy and sorrow of a brief but painful relationship: when she fell in love with her daughter's father while he was photographing bridges in her neighborhood. "When I'm at the low point of the dance, Zoot jumps up and taps me lightly on the nose as if to say, 'It's ok, it's just a game. You're not a little bird anymore.' And suddenly I feel so much stronger."

WHEN Sue's daughter, Selena, dances with Zoot, she seems guided by him to adopt rather awkward and momentarily frozen positions in the middle of her dance. The cat reacts to these still postures by leaping over and around her as if her sudden cessation of movement was quite unexpected and startling. Sue describes it as "a very playful interaction." Communication between cat and child appears to occur on some unconscious level, although Selena does respond directly to Zoot's tail movements. A cat's tail, unlike a dog's, is remarkably versatile in registering the most subtle nuances of mood and intention, and Selena can apparently "read" these signals. "Pussy's tail," she explains solemnly, "does wiggles that make me do I don't know why things."

*"Cats want to fly like fairies…"*

EITHER Zoot nor Oscar will dance at the same time with Selena. Each waits his turn and then tries to outperform the other, their leaps becoming increasingly frenetic and more elevated. Selena simply contends that "they want to fly like fairies." She adds, "Cats never ever eat fairies, except sometimes, by mistake."

ENID Blythe-Robinson has lived with Elgar since he was six weeks old. "Even as a kitten," she says, "he was exceptionally graceful." Dance critic Adam Bluestein agrees. "When he's dancing, his back lies in a deep curve, his legs and paws in harmonious gesture, while his tail is always delicately extended. He somehow manages to complete perfectly balanced *petit tours* while at the same time seeming to relate to his partner with an empathetic smile. Such startling virtuosity," concludes Bluestein, "suggests a connection with powerful inner forces." According to Enid, these "forces" are channelled through Elgar and released during the dance. The more graceful and at ease a cat is, the more peaceful and calming the energy received by its human dance partner will be. "I've tried dancing with cats who are just hopeless," she complains. "Overfed, bored felines who can't be bothered and others who just want to show off. They leap about, twisting this way and that without imparting any insight or spiritual depth at all!"

*"Such startling virtuosity suggests a connection with powerful inner forces."*  **63**

ENID claims Elgar possesses unseen healing powers. She discovered that when he slept on her bed at night it cured her insomnia. She also noticed that if she wrapped the light woollen shawl that Elgar slept on round her hands, her arthritic pain subsided for hours. "It's like he energizes the fibers in the shawl, and that stored-up energy seeps out and soothes your aches and pains for a while." She says it works on her woollen undergarments, too. "I sneak them under Elgar once he's asleep at night, and when I put them on in the morning, I feel a whole lot more supple and active in the hip department."

Elgar has a profound connection to the shawl he sleeps on. "It's almost as if it's a part of him," she says. "As soon as I take the shawl off the bed, he can't take his eyes off it. I lean down and start whispering, deliberately holding the shawl away from him. As soon as I hold it forth he stands up, and then he responds to every move I make. If I hold it upright, he stands upright; if I twirl it over, he twirls over; and if I shake it, he quivers from head to tail. Skeptics say he's just excited by it swishing about and me whispering, but he doesn't just jump after the shawl. He waits for each move to finish before he completes his. I believe it is a real interaction."

ALL cats are different when it comes to initiating a dance relationship. With Archie, a rather dim cat, Enid began by copying his movements. "Just like we do when we're forming a relationship with another human being," she explains, "we imitate each other. So when your cat sits, you sit; when it walks, you walk; and when it washes, you wash—same rhythm, same posture, same everything." She concedes certain grooming positions are challenging, but claims that, with practice, it's possible to achieve even some of the more rigorous ones. Once trust was established, Archie and Enid gradually coordinated their entire daily routines and progressed after six months from simple synchronized movements through to the first tentative dance steps.

ARVIN'S sessions with Missy are full on. "Most afternoons when the neighbors are at work, I pull down the shades, wind up some classic Springsteen, and we both bust out and go ballistic. It's ten minutes of high voltage and romp and stomp. Extreme twirling, jumping, and twisting. Really letting go, letting it out, and letting it in. It's better than any chemical substance because you're high on pure energy.

"Other cat dancers I've talked to on the Web use Heavy Metal, Techno, and World Beat. One guy says he uses Marley to build up such strong vibrational levels in just five minutes that they last for days. But you have to be careful; sometimes the energy is so powerful I worry about overstimulating my aura. At those levels, an unstable etheric oscillation could collapse into an astral vortex and suck my spiritual reserves into a state of negative sub-matter."

*"You're high on pure energy."*

*M*AX uses visualization and mime to inspire Wiky when they dance. "I'll think of a sparkling river, and before I've even begun to mime paddling down it, Wiky has become a leaping fish. That may make me think of a crocodile eating her, but just as I begin jaw snapping, she becomes a fluttering bird trying to distract me. It's a very stimulating technique, but you have to be careful. Once when we were dancing I visualized a bright red rose and then the fleeting image of a speeding red sports car entered my mind. At that very moment Wiky leapt sideways and crashed into the bookcase, which completely wrecked the dance sequence, not to mention one of my mother's vases. I've spoken to other dance visualizers about this and the general consensus is that she responded to the flower as a bee and then had no time to change roles when the sports car came along. Her only course was to take evasive action."

*"The cat's energy flows through me and helps me engage my real power."*   **71**

NVITING other people to watch you dance with your cat can be difficult at first," admits Max. "People who are only slightly skeptical can easily put the cat off. And sometimes Wiky just doesn't want to join in; and you can feel a bit stupid dancing around with somebody watching and the cat just sitting there. People are very polite when Wiky doesn't dance, but I know they think I'm crazy. Of course, when Wiky does perform they get terribly enthusiastic and want to bring their own cats over in the hope that she'll show them how to do it."

*B*ECAUSE some people feel awkward when they first begin dancing with their cats, Max has recently prepared a colorful set of cat-dancing affirmation cards. These, he says, are a useful first step in helping you to loosen up enough to tap into the feline vibration. *Completely relaxed, I lose myself in my cat. My cat's energy flows through me, and pulsates within me. My cat's energy helps me engage my real power. Cat dancing reveals the treasures of my unconscious.* Such affirmations can give first-time dancers the confidence they need to overcome self-conscious feelings that initially inhibit more advanced forms of human-feline interaction.

*I*N order to demonstrate how cats sense human depression and instinctively attempt to negate it, Arijá deliberately sets up a strong negative field around her. She does this by dressing in Gothic garb, playing droning music, and concentrating on deathly thoughts as she dances. Once the negativity reaches a particular intensity, Wiky reacts with an extraordinarily high leap that brings her cranial aura into contact with Arijá's and reverses the flow. Arijá believes that cats were used like this in medieval times to cure various forms of mental illness. Her opinion is echoed by psycho-historian Catherine Gollan, who notes that women were known to dance with cats as a means of building up energy states to positively influence various psychic processes. "Due to their seemingly magical abilities," she says, "these women were seen as evil witches, and they and their cats were persecuted by the Church because their actions challenged its claim to be the only body capable of performing miracles."

THE physical effect Toby's cat has on him suggests a very immediate transference of energy. "When Toffee rubs my legs," Toby says, "I feel all tingly and good in my tummy. It makes me want to jump." In fact, Toffee seems to invite Toby to dance by doing the most unusual twists and jumps all around him. "He's a real comedian," says Toby's mother. "He'll do some funny little stiff-legged walk and then stop and look at Toby, almost as if he's waiting for him to laugh. Their dances often start this way."

*"Toffee and I laugh at the same things."*

TOBY and Toffee exhibit a remarkable degree of synchronicity of movement and gesture. Toby's mother says their dances are too perfect for one to be copying the other. "They don't even look at each other when they're leaping about, and even if they did, there's just not enough time— they move too quickly to achieve that degree of coordination. His father agrees. "Sometimes you'd swear it was rehearsed, but it's not. And it's a completely different sequence every time."

Y mother says that Toffee and I must think the same to be able to dance like we do, but I don't know what Toffee thinks," says Toby. "I know we laugh at the same things, and I know he's got no other interests except dancing and that it makes him so tired he has to sleep all day. And I know he loves me."

*B*OB, Rose, and their cat, Felix, perform short story–dances for friends in their home. Here Felix plays Pinocchio in a work set to one of Chopin's nocturnes. Shadowed by the lame Fox, left, played by Rose, the hapless puppet jigs about woodenly while, above, Fox and blind Cat (Bob) introduce themselves to Pinocchio, who stupidly shows them his five gold coins.

ABYSSINIAN cats like Spike are lithe and sinuous with particularly well-developed slow-twitch muscle cells that enable them to hold a pose for long periods of time. This ability, which is vital for effective prey stalking, is also utilized by some cat dancers, who employ Fixed Position Stress (FPS) techniques to build up energy field vibrations. These dancers are interested in contained movements rather than expansive ones, and they often use just one single continuous note of music to complement them. Working with realistic preytoys, they train cats from an early age to hold crouched, ready-to-spring positions for extended periods of time. Then, by quickly getting into close physical proximity with the cat and assuming all aspects of its position exactly, dancers are able to resonate their energy fields with the cat's. This tends to induce a deep meditative calm rather than the euphoria produced by more rhythmic and expansive dance interactions. Once "contact" between human and feline has been established, more advanced upright positions can be achieved, with correspondingly heightened levels of awareness.

*"Cat dancing perfectly expresses the eloquence of pure form."*

*I*VAN uses five Abyssinians, all brothers and sisters from the same litter, for his FPS dancing. He begins with at least an hour of noncontact stroking and crouch mimicry to build resonance and then moves on to a brief period of advanced upright stretching. They end with a final leap to release the energy. When working with two cats, it is necessary to ensure negative and positive forces are balanced by checking that their tails are in opposing positions.

ANY yoga exercises are based on cat stretching and the calming effect of holding a pose. FPS dancers take this stretching and holding to an extreme by concentrating on contraction of the torso and straining of the limbs. When combined with feline interaction, this produces muscle quiver and the eventual etheric spasm necessary to induce deep levels of peace and tranquillity.

90

"When contact is made," says Ivan, "it's like I'm suddenly joined by a series of strings running from my limbs to the cat's. Even when we're in different positions, if I hold one arm up and the other down, he will, too. I'll pull a leg up, and he'll pull his up as well. But the synchronicity is so complete you can't be sure which one of us has initiated the action. Is it my leg that's doing the pulling or is it being pulled by his?"

THE particular pose Ivan and his cat choose is often dictated by the cat. During their preliminary warm-up, as they roll and rub together, the cat will frequently pay special attention to one area of Ivan's body. It will even curl up and try to sleep on it, no matter how uncomfortable. This is usually an area of high energy emanation that the cat is able to identify and apparently draw on. The cat's position tells Ivan the individual part of his body that is radiating most strongly and therefore what part he should force tension into in order to gain maximum energy build-up.

N a rare climactic moment, cats and human stretch in unison, hold the tension, and build energy levels to intoxicating heights of spiritual excitation. "In the final stages of an almost perfectly harmonized multicat dance," says Ivan, "the combined force of the feline vibration surges through me with such power, I'm able to step briefly from horizontal to vertical time. Afterward I feel incredibly alert and peaceful." But what do cats gain from the experience? Do they, as some believe, willfully charge up our energy fields so as to "feed off" them and selfishly enrich their own? Is that how cats maintain their poise and calm? Or are they actually trying to help us? Ivan believes that when we dance with cats, "We feed into a universal energy, enhance it, and give it back to the universe. So in the end," he says, "we all benefit."

# SELECTED BIBLIOGRAPHY

BECKER, R., and G. SELDEN. 1989. *The Body Electric*. Quill, San
Francisco.

CAPRA, F. *The Dance of Life.* Science Digest (no.4, 1982).

COPELAND, R., and C. MARSHALL. 1983. *What Is Dance*? Oxford
University Press, London.

FOGLE, B. 1997. *The Encyclopedia of the Cat*. Dorling Kindersley,
London.

GETTINGS, F. 1989. *The Secret Lore of the Cat*. Grafton Books, London.

GOOCH, S. 1981. *The Secret Life of Humans*. J. M. Dent, London.

GRANDIN, T. 1995. *Thinking in Pictures*. Doubleday, New York.

GROF, S. 1985. *Beyond the Brain*. State University of New York Press,
Albany, N.Y.

HALE, R. 1989. *The Witches' God: Lord of the Dance*. Phoenix, London.

HOGAN, L., D. METZER, and B. PETERSON, 1998. *Intimate Nature:
the Bond Between Women and Animals*. Fawcett Columbine, New York.

HUNT, V. 1995. *The Infinite Mind: The Science of Human Vibrations*.
Malibu Publishing Company, Malibu, Ca.

KARAGALLA, S., and D. KUNZ. 1989. *The Chakras and the Human
Energy Fields*. Quest Books, Wheaton, Ill.

MORRIS, D. 1987. *Catlore*. Crown Publishers, New York.

PEAT, D. 1987. *Synchronicity: The Bridge between Mind and Matter*.
Bantam Books, New York.

SMITH, P. 1989. *Animal Talk: Interspecies Telepathic Communication*.
Pegasus Publications, Point Reyes Station, Ca.

STEPHENS, G. 1990. *Legacy of the Cat*. Chronicle Books, San Francisco.

More information on dancing with cats can be found on the Web
site of the Museum of Non-Primate Art at:

**http://www.netlink.co.nz/~monpa**

# ACKNOWLEDGMENTS

Planning, research, photography, and writing for this book have taken three
years to complete. We are deeply indebted to the many people who have
given so generously of their time and knowledge during this period. In
particular we would like to mention; Jessica Ahipene, Ivan Arrdon, Lindsay
Auger, Kevin & Val Ball, Robert Sedcole Bargh, Peter Belfor, Enid Blythe-
Robinson, Ros Brittain, Polly Buring, Rose & Bob Butcher, Francesca da
Souza-Silver, Arijá, Bill & Brân Davies, Vicky & John Fletcher, Ayesha
Furlong, Fred Furrow, Max Green, Toby Gumby, Gwyneth & John Halson,
Victoria Hamilton, Andé Handyside, Gregg Harris, Chris Hone, Brian
Hotter, Helen House, Ann Hunt, Margaret & Susanne Jackson, Lauren
Langford, Sandee, Elden & Len Lidbetter, Ralph D. McAllister, Jeanne
Macaskill, Trevor Morris, Alistair Mullis, Martin O'Connor, Pip Payne,
Daphne Pringle, Jan Ratcliff, Rick & Dianne Renner, Michelle
Richecoeur, Sabine Rogge, Kathryn Saville, Sue & Selena Slingle, Jane
Spilt, Joy & Jill Tilt, Linda Topp, Marvin Weed, Stephanie Weinrauch, Paul
& Tony Van Zanten, & The Christchurch Polytechnic School of Feline Art
& Dance.